WHAT MAKES AN AMPHIBIAN?

THE ANIMAL KINGDOM

Lynn M. Stone

The Rourke Book Co., Inc.
Vero Beach, Florida 32964

PHOTO CREDITS
All photos © Lynn M. Stone except p.21 © Breck P. Kent

EDITORIAL SERVICES:
Penworthy Learning Systems

Library of Congress Cataloging-in-Publication Data

Stone, Lynn M.
  What Makes an Amphibian? / by Lynn M. Stone.
    p. cm. — (The Animal Kingdom)
  Includes index
  Summary: Discusses the habits, bodies, and different kinds of
amphibians and their relationships with people.
    ISBN 1-55916-191-4
    1. Amphibians—Juvenile literature. [1. Amphibians] I. Title II.
Series: Stone, Lynn M.   Animal Kingdom.
QL644.2.S77 1997
597.8—dc21   96–52191
                                                            CIP
                                                            AC

Printed in the USA

TABLE OF CONTENTS

AMPHIBIANS

Frogs, toads, and salamanders are amphibians. Amphibians are one of the groups of **vertebrate** (VER tuh BRAYT) animals—animals with backbones. Fish, reptiles, birds, and mammals are also vertebrates.

Amphibians differ from other vertebrates in one or more ways. Most amphibians, for example, begin their lives in water. As adults they can live on land.

Amphibians have soft bodies covered only by skin, which is usually moist. Amphibians don't have scales, fur, or feathers.

Amphibians like moisture, but most kinds are at home out of water as well as in it.

HABITS OF AMPHIBIANS

Amphibians are **cold-blooded** (KOLD BLUD ed). Their body temperature changes with the air or water temperature around them. Amphibians cannot live in extreme heat or cold.

On hot days amphibians seek cool, damp hiding places. They escape cold or dry weather by burrowing into the ground. There they stay inactive, waiting for warmer or wetter weather.

Many amphibians are most active on warm, rainy nights. Then they travel from land to water to find mates.

Northern toads attract mates on wet spring nights by calling loudly through balloonlike throat sacs.

KINDS OF AMPHIBIANS

Scientists have listed about 3,200 kinds, or **species** (SPEE sheez), of amphibians. Most of them are frogs and toads. Toads are basically frogs with dry, warty skin.

Salamanders make up about 300 species. Salamanders have long, cigar-shaped bodies.

Many salamanders have no lungs. They breathe through their skin. A few species breathe through **gills** (GILZ).

Legless **caecilians** (suh SIL yunz) are the third group of amphibians. None of the 150 species lives in Canada or the United States.

This young newt lives on land. As an adult, though, it will live in water. Most amphibians follow an opposite life path.

WHERE AMPHIBIANS LIVE

Amphibians need water or moist conditions to keep from drying out. They live in places with damp, mild climates.

Most kinds of adult amphibians spend time on land and in fresh water. A few spend most of their adult lives in underground burrows.

Some species of salamanders live in water. They breathe through gills, like fish.

Amphibians live on every continent except icy Antarctica.

This grotto salamander doesn't need to see because it lives in a Missouri cave.

The toad's rough skin, unusual among the smooth-skinned amphibians, does not cause warts.

Amphiumas rarely leave water, but the one at lower left did. Now it's prey for a sandhill crane.

THE BODIES OF AMPHIBIANS

Amphibians are little creatures, the smallest of vertebrates. They are rarely longer than six inches (about 15 centimeters) or heavier than two ounces (57 grams).

The largest North American amphibian is an **aquatic** (uh KWAT ik) salamander, the amphiuma. Aquatic animals spend their lives in water. The amphiuma can be almost four feet (about one meter) long.

Amphibians generally have four legs. Some salamanders have only two legs. Others are eel-like. They have no legs!

Some amphibians can change skin color to match their surroundings.

This lungless salamander in a Georgia brook breathes through its skin.

AMAZING AMPHIBIANS

Many amphibians are amazing creatures. Some tree frogs never leave their treetop homes. They lay their eggs in little leaf cups of water.

The world's largest amphibian, the Japanese giant salamander, may be longer than you at five feet (one and one-half meters).

In South American rain forests, poison-arrow frogs are both colorful and deadly. Their bodies make poison that **native** (NAY tiv) peoples use on arrowheads.

Toads are not so amazing that they can cause warts. Their skin can leak a mild poison, though.

Cute but deadly, a poison-arrow frog's bright colors may warn predators away.

PREDATOR AND PREY

Most amphibians are **predators** (PRED uh terz). They catch each other and smaller animals to eat. Most of their **prey** (PRAY) are insects.

Some amphibians also eat larger animals, such as fish, birds, other amphibians, and little furry animals.

Amphibians usually capture prey with their sticky tongues. A few species have sharp teeth.

Amphibians are prey as well as predators. In North America, fish, otters, minks, herons, cranes, pelicans, and many other animals eat frogs, toads, and salamanders.

An earthworm falls prey to a hungry tiger salamander.

BABY AMPHIBIANS

Amphibians hatch from jellylike masses of eggs that are usually laid in water.

Most newborn amphibians are squirmy, fishlike **larva** (LAHR vuh), or tadpoles. They breathe through gills. They look very little like adult frogs, toads, and salamanders.

In time, the bodies of tadpoles change. Young frogs, for example, lose their fishlike tail. They develop lungs and legs. Soon they can walk out of the water and breathe air.

Wood frog tadpole shows early signs of becoming an adult—hind legs.

PEOPLE AND AMPHIBIANS

Most people never meet many of the amphibians in their neighborhoods. Amphibians live mostly secret lives. They hide in ponds, streams, soft soil, and damp leaves.

Often, though, people hear the trills, buzzes, croaks, and honks of frogs and toads.

Amphibians are helpful to people because they eat insects. People can help amphibians by protecting the woods and wet places where they live.

Glossary

aquatic (uh KWAT ik) — of the water; living on or in the water

caecilians (suh SIL yunz) — group of amphibians without legs

cold-blooded (KOLD BLUD ed) — refers to animals whose body temperature stays about the same as that of their surroundings; fish, amphibians, and reptiles

gills (GILZ) — organs that help fish and certain other animals breathe by taking oxygen from water

larva (LAHR vuh) — an early stage of life in amphibians and certain other animals

native (NAY tiv) — a person whose ancestors were among the very early people who lived in a place

predator (PRED uh ter) — an animal that hunts other animals for food

prey (PRAY) — an animal that is hunted by another animal for food

species (SPEE sheez) — within a group of closely related animals, one certain kind, such as a *leopard* frog

vertebrate (VER tuh BRAYT) — an animal with a backbone; a fish, amphibian, reptile, bird, or mammal

INDEX